I SUGAR THE BONES

Juana Adcock

Out-Spoken Press
London

Published by Out-Spoken Press,
PO Box 78744
London, N11 9FG

A CIP record for this title is available from the British Library.

First edition published 2024
ISBN: 9781068671203

Typeset in Futura and Adobe Caslon
Design by Patricia Ferguson
Printed and bound by Short Run Press

Out-Spoken Press is supported using public funding by the National
Lottery through Arts Council England.

ARTS COUNCIL
ENGLAND

Supported using public funding by

I SUGAR THE BONES

CONTENTS

CARTOON COUNTRIES

CARTOON LOVE

FIRE TRIPTYCH

≠

'But how, if we live enclosed by stone
In a dark and treeless valley of walls?'

—Cesário Verde
tr. Richard Zenith

'all symmetry an excuse
for keeping count'

—Meena Kandasamy

'I am the body kneeling at the river's edge
letting it drink from me'

—Natalie Diaz, *Postcolonial Love Poem*

≠

CARTOON COUNTRIES

IN SPRINGFIELD, MEXICO, LISA SIMPSON SPEAKS IN SPANISH

SCENE I. LISA SIMPSON SPEAKS OF THE DUBBING ACTOR
WHO VOICED HER FOR LATIN AMERICA

Many people don't know this
since I wear pearls round my neck
like an upper class 1950s North American teen
and my skin is crayoned in an invisible hue
that does not at first glance
appear to signal *meaning*

but for most of my life I was voiced
by Patricia Acevedo Limón.
A career woman in Mexico City,
brown eyes, brown skin
bowl haircut, statement jewellery
reminiscent of indigenous cultures.

Despite the success of the show
she never flaunted my name.
Instead she gave interviews
at deserted stalls in obscure
Mexican comic book conventions
did her own housework and rode the bus.

While still very young
she attended a voice-over school
that taught her to make her voice more palatable
to a wider Latin American audience.
How to use neutral words
in an *unmarked* accent

how to push her timbre
to the back of her palatoglossal arch

1

in the style of the Spaniards
to the edge of her oropharynx
as far back as she could
to furthermost corner of the head

while still revealing a tender emotion
the way women are expected from birth
to take up as little space as possible
even within our own physical structure

SCENE 2. LISA SIMPSON WRITES A DIARY ENTRY ABOUT HER
TRANS EX

After my lover left
to become a woman
(she had always felt like one
she said, just couldn't tell me)
a wound I dared not speak of
began to mushroom
revealing its three-fold nature:
(a) that my gendered body
was made to carry *more than*
(to carry children! Ed Sheeran blurts out
from his cameo in a hot air balloon)
(b) that god had made my body
as a mere *companion to*, and
(c) that god had proclaimed my body
to be *his temple*: that to transform it
would be a sin.
Or so it was believed
even as we continued
to diet and exercise
hair dye and shellac
extensions and filler.
Besides all this, there was,
in my lover's parting
a whiff of heteronormativity:
that I had not been gentle
not sweet enough
(ie, not enough of a woman)
to allow a person to become
in my company the woman
they always dreamed of.
But I would have journeyed with her
to the end of the earth

3

Incidentally, Patricia Acevedo Limón
also voiced Sailor Moon—that starry-eyed
most definitively blonde drama queen

who somehow managed to command armies
by harnessing what Brené Brown would call
the power of vulnerability.

Not to labour the point but Brown
may be key for if Brené had not been white
she may have noticed this power

is more difficult to wield when you are not
a princess at birth. Rarely do you become one
even if you marry Prince Harry or work

three times as hard in the workplace, at home
and in therapy learning techniques
of *leaning in, self-compassion, radical acceptance.*

White-passing or not we do as Brown says
following the recipe to a tee the way
a foreigner might attempt authentic molé:

ten hours toasting and grinding
nuts seeds chilies cacao to achieve a substance
that no Mexican has ever attempted at home.

With near-perfect execution we
reveal ourselves difficult emotional women
who are hard work yet self-possessed

in the way that led Sailor Moon
to her heroic success.
The techniques never worked for me

but I was able to harness instead
the power of invisibility
and I was granted access

to the palaces of power.
I swear, I could just drive right in.

Even in my dented white Shadow
that hadn't been washed for months, in my cheap
clothes from Del Sol, my nails and my roots not done.

Because I was white enough, I dreamed
I could leave and was able to leave.
I simply drove away from my place

in the order of things

For the rest there is something about viewing the West
that comes in strange anachronistic terms
like watching *Lost in Space* or *Gilligan's Island*
always in black and white, forty years or so after
they first aired. We still had black and white TVs
and to me, everyone in Springfield was variously tinted
their provenance unmarked. The donut-devouring
policeman was descendant of neither masters nor slaves.
A neutral Latin American voice gave nothing away.
The bar tender, Mou, read as Afro-Latino, based on his hair
slender frame and stern tones. Those pale twins were
albinos, not Asian, and the shopkeeper's accent
was stereotypical of nothing. Even when he dressed up
as a cowboy, and spoke in a slightly grammatically incorrect
Norteño Mexican Spanish, it was not possible to convey
the implications of the joke.
Nor was the angry janitor sufficiently Scottish
in a way that required no context.
He was simply deranged
and occasionally wore Scottish clothes

Many may not remember this, but to support myself
through university, I rose each morning at 5:00 am
to teach private English lessons to a decrepit señor Burns.

He desperately needed to improve his language skills
but he was high enough in rank, and I young enough, white enough
to be considered beautiful, so all he wanted to do was talk to me

in bed for hours about his life, his wife, his longings.
I never did go to bed with him, but in his attempt
he opened up to me about his secrets

his childhood dreams and his youth
his years as a manager in Colombia at the height of the drug war
and that time his wife was kidnapped on her way to church.

Even to this day their extra king size bed was not wide enough
for how much she needed to be held. He slept right on the edge
of the mattress as if trying to escape his fate.

He drove me to campus in his fancy car,
promised a good job upon graduation, gifted me
an expensive watch for Valentine's Day

which I did not accept
since my boyfriend might suspect
as he often did

though I was faithful to him
even in my wildest dreams
about the Portuguese boy.

Later, when I mentioned I needed money
señor Burns handed me a couple of hundred-dollar bills
straight from his wallet. Which was a lot of money

when Springfield was in Mexico.
He soon requested a new teacher
to replace me.

I never told anyone but the reason I needed money then
was to travel 600 miles across the border
to where it was legal to end a pregnancy.

There are no words I can say about this, only the sadness
of not being enough – not to a country, the law
parents, bosses, professors,

my promising career – not to my boyfriend,
my friends, myself or even my unborn,
tiny as it was –

not, as Reverendo Alegría claimed
the size of a grain of rice, but cluster of cells
visible only under a microscope

or under a sorrow wide enough for no child
to ever deserve

SCENE 6. WE SEE HER PLAYING SAXOPHONE ON THE BRIDGE

My saxophone teacher was called Tommy Rodríguez,
a jazz pioneer born in Tuxpan, Veracruz.

Our baseball team was from a place
where there has never been segregation:

many African American players made their careers here.
It may seem like ours was an enlightened society

we always said race does not exist
but mom, dad, do you remember

how you forbade me from seeing my boyfriend
because he was not white enough?

You never said as much, since we lived in grayscale
but wasn't that the true reason why you didn't trust him?

Why you never let him in the front door?
We used to sit on the front steps with our dog *Huesos*

to kiss in the shadows

My dad was voiced by Humberto Vélez
an abundant and charming man.
His timbre was full and unself-conscious
in that uniquely Latino way.

He was paid fifty-two dollars
per recorded episode.

(On average it takes two full days
to dub twenty-two minutes
of lip-synched animation
before the voice gives in to fatigue.)

After fifteen years of wildly successful work
he was undercut by a non-unionised actor
who could afford to earn
a lower wage on fewer benefits.

In those years, dubbing studios were cropping up
in poorer Spanish-speaking countries
and the Mexican studios needed to cut costs
to remain competitive.

The man who voiced my dad
said he never liked to get political.
That all he knew how to do was to act.
But he could not accept the new contract.

How would he support his family?
He did all he could but in the end
the union lost the fight and our voices
instantly recognisable to 600 million people

were all replaced. Though we had been known
and loved throughout the continent
with our neutral Latin American accents
and our distinctive personalities and affect

the company saw this fit.
I don't know how many noticed the slight shift
the vague imitation
from inexperienced actors.

But I keep tucking my voice
neatly behind my ears
like the temple tips
of a pair of comedy glasses.

Keeping my pain to myself
for everyone to see

SAN YSIDRO CROSSING

Have you been to that border town,
the place where nothing is?

A half-city, half-mall
choking on its
idea of itself.

Its cardboard box imitation
of haciendas and Spanish baroque
painted the colour of sunset and plunder.

In a motel room, the only lighting
comes from the billboards outside
as they reach their tendrils

into all that is soft in me.
On my last night in Tijuana
I read a message on the wall:

to never arrive
is to already be there with you

SELF-SERVE SLURPEE

Driving across the radio stations
I hear locutores de San Diego urging
us all the way to Ensenada:
>Text WEALTH to 333-111

Peddler-entrepreneurs take advantage
of sun and traffic jam to sell ripped music
on USB sticks and cold drinks from an icebox
en la camioneta parked on the hard shoulder.

A child is writing something in the dirt with a stick.

We inch forward the interference gives way
to a man singing his masculinities in Spanish:
you deserve to be treated with respect to be loved
in a way that I'm unable to love I lust for you one day,

I'm cold-hearted the next and I don't know why it's just
who I am and I can't change I'll take it to my grave
I'm a cruel man I can't tell the difference between my love
and your pain
>Text WEALTH to 333-111

Marching bands on hire for declarations of love.
Tambores y trombones blaring at the couple
bailando en la playa. She was smiling, head back,
hair black like a waterfall.

What you're asking of me is impossible I wasn't born to be king
or a prince. You want my feet on the ground I'll always be soaring
my love like the eagle. Remember how many times I said to you
how often you were warned

The riverbed is fortified in concrete, straight, lifeless transit.
It's what they do to rivers in America. The road signs keep giving
the option to return to San Diego, or keep taking wrong
turns in the carrousel that Tijuana is.

Have you thought of making changes in your life
to make things easier for yourself? Find out who you are
and where you come from with our $200 DNA test.
I'll tell you who you are for free, I reply.
        Text WEALTH to 333-111

A Mexican radio presenter now:
¿Cómo está la línea para cruzar?
Está de una hora y media por la Sentri.
They call it 'crossing the line' here.

Where I'm from we call it 'crossing the bridge'
like Samhain's veil between two worlds
the river becomes vertical see-through whether full
or dried up.

An infinitely long object with no width, depth
or curvature a line exists only in one dimension.
We call it La Línea because of the long waiting in queues
to cross a line marked in steel fencing.

In our eighties Datsun, in the sun the lines
– which Euclid called a breadthless length –
had depth as well as duration and always seemed
to last all morning.

American border patrols with names like
'Carlos Gonzalez' (accent missing from the second 'a')
would not speak to us in Spanish. A rush of adrenaline

every time being treated like key suspects
though we were just popping across
to buy a couple of those self-serve slurpees.

≠

200 km from the border the couple in the hotel room
next to mine argue in Spanish. When they switch to English
stepping into their perfect American accents she becomes bolder,
more assertive, and he quieter.

After some slamming and shuffling he returns to the room
in Spanish, louder now, macho. This goes on son la envidia
de los amigos. They have rented their own private
chunk of the beach to do this.

The sign outside our rooms says: Playa cerrada.
Agua contaminada. Evite contacto con el agua hasta nuevo aviso

STORYLINES

Roads are heavier on the other side of the line.
Asphalt mixed with cement is whiter. Loudening
under car wheels, it hardens over time, requiring
little maintenance.

The dwellings are transient, wooden-framed
lighter as if to be filled with cushions and the crinkle
of food wrappers. Some child's quiet voice in a corner
of the room mouthing *and I'll huff and I'll puff.*

This set design these theatre props. On this side
of the line the asphalt grows crocodile-skinned.
Pockmarked and permeable it copes with earthquakes
forms wave-like furrows in the heat.

Initially it's cheaper to lay but has a shorter lifespan.
Our houses, however, you can tell by just looking
have a different weight to them in contrast to the timber
preferred by the anglophones.

We like our structures built heavy as pyramids
as if to keep us here a while longer

WINDOWS NORTH OF THE RIVER

The shop windows were widened
to display happy customers as merchandise
highlighting our outsideness
as we are unable to enter

not having that kind of capital
or way to belong

STORY OF STEEL

I place my palm en la reja called 'border wall'
let its steel enter my body: iron alloyed with carbon
hardened to prevent the *movement of dislocations*.

The body of an adult human contains four grams
of iron. All four of mine rush to meet la reja imantada.
When we speak of magnetism we think of love

charisma or crowds of faces in one direction
but never of iron as the metal at the active site
of many enzymes dealing with cellular respiration.

Glasgow's sandstone tenements contain the red
of iron. Our blood stone is iron ore. It emanates
its own light against the wall of cloud refracting sun.

I am the blood migrating bringing cargo from one cell
to the next keeping the body alive I transport
mercancía maquinaria metralletas manos.

The iron for the wall was mined in the M states
bordering with Canada. Many years ago, the land
was cleared of its people, wildlife and forests.

Migrants from northern Europe fed the logs
down the rivers laid the train tracks peeled away
layers of life bloodlet the earth to build

a line of steel marking the limits of possession
a breadthless length to create transit and scarcity
division and dreams

STORY OF THE LETTER M

With a prophet's moustache and a penchant for conspiracy
the madman explains to me that language is a form of mind control

the grammar itself holding us in a mudra an incantation
muttered over millennia by our mothers, shaping our thoughts

I want to master the art of the pictogram, he says, earliest form
of writing uncontaminated by the misers, the drive for accumulation

manufactured with the rise of agriculture the letter M, for example
is from the pictogram of a wave we forget where it comes from

it loses all meaning we write it over and over without ever thinking
of water or how mar y mother, muro y morada, music and moon

mareo y marea are of one essence.

As he speaks, I watch the surfers gliding along the lip of the perfect
breakers almost for the whole line of the horizon before they topple

over into the sea like tiny plastic soldiers.
That night we slept hearing the waves crash onto the rocks.

In the morning, we were rocks too. Our hearts hardened lava.
The Pacific had smoothed round windows through us

like a Barbara Hepworth sculpture we were made whole
by what we lacked

STORY OF JACOB BAEGART

In his 1768 love letter to Baja California
the missionary Jacob Baegart wrote:

just as their skin is their dwelling
and they never fear losing their home
the furniture there can neither be damaged
by moths nor stolen by thieves the mountains
are their walls and libraries the starry night
is their chandeliered ceiling with these riches
and pleasures they spend their lives in health
and greater serenity and joy than those who
know no end to their possessions

STORY OF TRANSFERENCE

a Scottish migrant's American empire of steel
a caravan walks alongside a rust-red wall

bodies carry the others' load
across el Río Bravo, the River Grande

a shared river, bilingual in name
divvying up the water's dividends

a Freudian slip, a fear
that knows no delineation

repressed and expelled from the self
projected outside the fence

an othering of despair
a phantom boat

a border with an insecurity complex
a military-industrial complex

children in cages
wrapped in tin foil

jornaleros or the highly skilled
from a 'crime-infested' nation

day labourers shipped in and out
to build illegally on their land

'human animals,' 'rapists,' 'thugs'
'targets' neutralised, soft skulls sniped

unclear where freedom lies
but we are safe behind the gates

resources extracted
wealth transferred

border shut down to trade
a million crossings per day

mutually benefitting an alien concept
to the immured

el río sigue llevando

AFTER BANKSY (EVERYBODY WANTED TO BUY A PLOT OF LAND IN PARADISE)

With the nearest airport just thirty minutes away
the sand was white as sugar the waves
refracted like a precious gem the turtles
could still be swum with

(though now there was a queue)
and the value of property was set to rise
faster than the levels of the ocean
that the city was built to overlook.

Both jungle and holy land as concepts
remained lush. Our parents were rich
and the workplace was changing:
our dreams were no longer remote.

The main square featured
hideous public art
and a pious little chapel
with an altar-fountain

and walls made of heart vines
to make us think of love.
And for the amusement of all
a night market and fair

where some displaced indigenous people
had been granted a permit
to perform their ritual dances
out of season every night

and beg for change

23

THE DREAM OF REASON PRODUCES MONSTERS

If a wall of such magnitude exists there must be a danger of equal proportions on the other side. Savage, bloodthirsty mercenaries that kill without a second thought. Or a place where human life is too cheap. But the idea of the other side is ambiguous. Who is captive, and who is free? When Jean Valjean climbed over the wall with Cosette on his shoulders to cross Paris with a passport that marked him as an ex-convict was the wall rendered obsolete or was it built higher in a different place? The wall has no continuity, does not loop round or join up at the other end. The wall has gaps but they are where nobody is looking. The geography also helps. Hills conceal. Roads wind around. More than to prevent transit the wall serves to communicate the idea of danger.
The wall itself is
propaganda

STORY OF MILITARY AS AUTOIMMUNE DISEASE

Chewing my tongue into a wall of flesh hundreds of pounds
of pressure my jaw clenches my cheeks harden biting off
masticating pieces of myself biting back the words I might say
my body rebels against me or do I rebel against it, who has the
right? do I have the right to resist my body? does my body have
the right to defend itself? do you condemn my body for wanting
to live the wall of flesh on my chest cement fortified with steel
security cameras all along protecting my watchtowers as I chew
down flesh and it gets stuck in my throat leaving an acidic taste
lodged in my jaw clenching to salivate to smear for money my
cells hurtle to their compulsion's content stolen organs eyes
shut as they pray to money my cells shut eyes as they shatter
stolen skin shrouded in blue plastic ditches live burial ziptied
tank tire print spilled guts minted as money my cells shut eyes
and drop bombs on myself then celebrate for money we must
destroy the hornets' nest say the health ministers as my cells
drop bombs on my cells this is good the ministers say as they
starve my cells to a skeleton the hypocritical oath: first, do no
harm that is seen help with one hand press the bomb into the
body with another I sob and I masticate grey ash paste forms
under my eyes where saltwater should be I am the grey paste in
my sandals sweat mixed with ash as I hold my pee and we claw
through the rubble of my body following the stench of rotting
flesh my cells race through bombed streets along the din of one
continuous horn to a smeared hospital floor my body half-open
half-carbonized still breathing my cells bomb the hospitals
bomb the orphanages bomb the meaning out of meaning bomb
my cells in mismatched sandals in a ten hour queue my cells
carving the star of david onto the cheeks of my cells with a
knife and filming it for money my body bombing itself I walk
through the park in autumn then winter then all the way to the

end of spring how am I still alive I must be made of steel I hope
I never live to see another summer says my body as it poisons
the land salts the water infests the air determined to choke itself
for money to ensure not a single body plant animal protozoa
phosphate solubilizing bacteria can live again for money what's
better than pine needles killing the forest floor deep sea mining
killing everything we know for money for fifty years of boom-
and-bust prosperity lost to money for dead land bloodied fingers
scrolling endless through the feed I starve myself feed myself on
images of my body crushed under the rafters my dry palm leaves
covered in ash my cells bring their hands to their head tearing
out hairs as I heave useless wails the whole forest heaving
with me in lacrimation on the river a duck swimming against
current pushing itself forward head back and forth in the same
absurd bobbing movement as my chest expelling moans my jaw
clenched the solid wall of flesh around a consciousness
contracted strong as fortified cement begins
to crack

MOUNTAIN ROAD

you
      drunk at the wheel
                  telling me that
                        fear is
                              poisoning our bodies

me
      body fake-relaxed
                  eyes running along the edge
                              of the cliff

                  as we draw   hairpin curves
                              round the distant
                                    smoke
                              of
                  villages

the disappeared signal
of mothers'
lugged firewood
      their strength

the particulates   suspended
rising skywards
as if to offer up
in sacrifice

≠

the healer
                              cigarette hanging from his mouth
        runs the sahumerio bowl along my arms and legs
doodling smoke crosses and hoops
to cleanse my body
                        of the countless calcified apprehensions
                    thinning the veil
before we enter

The paved highway we left
behind is smoke. The copal
burning is the way ahead.
The incensed mountains of
plastic waste are burning up
the rungs of some hell we
created. Our lungs are filling
with that waste. I take a drag
the embers redden lighting
the darkness around my face.
In the cold mornings this is
the only thing that warms us.
The nicotine swirls between
nictations and we leave
no trace of ourselves but
the faintest feather of grey
already vanishing before we
have made out its shape

STEP UP, LITTLE SPIRITS

Life liked to partake in the picnic
and we didn't like that.

We prefer death—spread
concrete on the jungle

all surfaces homogenised smoothed out
so we can have 42 brands of rice cooker

bras in 27 different shades of green
plastic buckets, entire aisles of them

so many things that we cannot name them all
in a place without sidewalks

(walking is considered barbaric
in this heat).

But we've kept the tiny staircases
for the little spirits to step up into their shrines.

A French man was surprised by this. 'You don't have
spirits in France?' I asked. 'No, we are rationalists.'

I worried for the spirits in Europe
unable to find rest

still on the north wind that blaws doon the years
come the howls and the cries of the ghosts of Red Clyde
—Alistair Hulett & Dave Swarbrick

IN A WAY, ENCLOSED BY ITS CONTAINER WALL, THE RIVER CLYDE IS

a strip mine. Useful lifespan
approximately 150 years
its value all extracted now.
Yet the dredged silt still
hangs ghostlike in the veins
of the city left around it.
Which lights up each night
like an amusement park
no for one. For spirits
wandering in a Miyazaki film

fordable. At low tide the water's depth
was less than the span
of my shoulders. At high tide
the cold surface licked
just above my breasts.
Yon ocht inches ahint tha toon
eight small islands in the river
where trees and villagers lived.
Gather up your skirts and
push a paddle boat out

a razed temple. An earlier belief
system and way of life
destroyed to make way
for new doctrine. Clerics
giving up poverty vows
approve of exploitation

30

for profit. The land
is hollowed out to fill
a power vacuum created
by distant legal transferences

a map of 1759. Men had barely
learned how to draw
straight lines on paper
and already were determined
to *'cleanse, scour, straighten
and improve'* a defenceless
natural shape. Joy removed.
Entanglements cut. Witches
executed. In the name
of progress

affordable. Child's play. A mathematical
solution in a two-dimensional
world. *Flatland*, before
Edwin Abbott Abbott had
written his novella about a world
built in two dimensions.
Cyclical time deemed
unscientific and straightened
to resemble a canal
for the transit of goods

fake news. A daemonologie written
to glorify an orphaned man
who strives for power in
lieu of – boring but true –
the love he never received.
Panic-induced populace
thirsty for sensation. The devil
may even be within you.
Stay vigilant. Destroy
all that is sensuous

31

an investment plan. The sum of ecological
　　　　resources squandered
　　　　way back at the beginning.
　　　　A present where nothing lives.
　　　　Where seagulls scan dronelike
　　　　for chip trails on the drunken
　　　　paths of the fourth generation
　　　　unemployed. Thriving in the
　　　　chemical waste that sixty years on
　　　　still seeps

a simulation of the Clyde. The Clyde
　　　　imagining all the things the
　　　　Clyde could be if the Clyde
　　　　were not the Clyde. Or if
　　　　the Clyde were located
　　　　in a more geographically
　　　　advantageous position.
　　　　Like a place where existing
　　　　trade routes converge,
　　　　or anywhere south

an abandoned factory. Its scale
　　　　too vast for human
　　　　comprehension
　　　　with no longer
　　　　any conceivable use.
　　　　A paradise for squatters.
　　　　Bolt cutters in hand we
　　　　swim, sail, hold races
　　　　all-night parties. Barriers
　　　　knocked down

ripe for reclamation. Who truly
owns this hindering
of transit through our oon
haime, these useless docking
bays? Soon vegetation
softening the bricks, heated
pools, laughter, music, wild-
life, fishing, floating markets
street food, whatever the
weather. Unticketed

overflowing. Flooding our living
rooms. Forcibly made
to carry, coming in
with a vengeance.
Our bodies absorb
the excess damp, our minds
plagued by the scarcity.
Now we are the ones needing
dredged. All we can do is pray
to the Clyde. It says: play

its own arisings. Volcanic rock
blasted and disposed of
at the edges. Energy made
sluggish. Despite constant
rain the sensation there
is always bone-dry. Mud-
cakes cooked in the sun
in Haiti. The mud is mixed
with salt, margarine and
water, making it good to eat

a plantation. Species removed
to make way for the monocrop.
Indigenous peoples enslaved
and dressed in tartan.
The Highland Clearances
with so many displaced
were done first in the Caribbean.
An African queen caged
nominally free. Still grappling
with police brutality

plastic money. Poured in
from abroad. Forests
of glitzy glass and steel
buildings. An imitation
of an imitation of luxury.
The rot painted over
to appear sleek in brochures.
Ignoring, then commodifying
the value generated
by us who live here

a theologian. With his head
in the clouds, bent over
written words, he crawls
under the edge of the sky.
Tells us he has found
the place where heaven
and earth meet.
Disregarding the realities
of everyday life, he seeks
the Truth

a mirror. Needing no words
        metaphors or comparisons.
        Patiently waiting each day
        yet rarely fully seen.
        Blinded by its own past
        shying away from its own
        reflection. All emotions
        denied, it snags
        on sentimental narrative
        to hide away its grief

a rape survivor. Flesh cut open
        to accommodate steamships
        driven through still reeling
        unable to feel pain.
        Cities and rivers were once
        thought not to.
        The size of their earnings
        still a measure of adulthood.
        And so the infantilised
        'poor'

a Scold's bridle. Now removed.
        Though the tongue
        is lacerated and numb.
        The spirit roams homeless.
        The malaise resulting
        from eviction was called
        addiction. Though we
        were hunted down
        our records dispersed
        our names forgotten, we know

an artificial respirator. Giving no
    thought to the future.
    It is only here for this breath.
    Now this one. Now this one.
    Walled up and contained
    in a sterilised environment.
    Rendered sterile: unable
    to reproduce or create life.
    Kept alive by external forces.
    That is, by us

bodies deemed disposable. Fed
    to the apparatus of war.
    A harvesting site for cannon
    fodder. We were always highly
    skilled in the arts that only
    love can be competent at.
    Work which can never
    be repaid with money.
    Half-heartedly lionised
    as essential. Clap clap clap

ordinary people. Left to our own
    devices. Mutual aid
    as the only path to survival.
    Which means tending
    to those closest to us
    as Arvo Pärt said in an interview
    not reported by the British press.
    We had forgotten. The whole
    point of earning a living
    was to look after each other

a candle. Humbly lit at night.
A companion in solitary
as we switch off the lights
of propaganda. Becoming
rich in time for thought
pleasure and conversation.
The flame, in its irregularity
grows dim and cool at times
then warms bright again. Just
a tempo

a city. No longer held back.
No longer *'kept under*
by the shallowness of her river.'
No longer drowned
by the disquieting depths
of prosperity. So-called

SUGARBUILT

We
turn the page
and it all crumbles:
a majestic grand siécle   staircase built of sugar
towering obelisks   panelled domes
baroque   ceilings
built   of sugar
pillars
stucco plants and shells
in arabesques   cartouches
of sugar   delicate
latticework   of sugar
priests giving   sugar sermons
in pulpits
of sugar   in overly
ornate   churches
of sugar   as the sun
pours in through the stunning
stained sugar glass
the granulated
salt-like
powder
on the table
the silver spoons made of sugar served with
tea in translucent sugar china decorated in intricate sugarwork
quadruple-tier cakes iced with Louis XV florets of gold-plated sugar
plaster sprinkled with sugardew doublelayer sugarfilo pilasters
laced in spiderthread-thin sugardoilies topped
with tiny sugarcreamed melt-in-your-mouth sugarbirds
and a snow-white sugarglaze steeped in
sugartrade centuries
sweet

HOGWEED

Sinking stuck from the shoulders down:
a half-sunken dog, as in the Goya painting
though it's unclear if it should be a gerund
sinking in this moment, in sand or in water

or sunken as in boat
or sunken as in an eye
brimming with the selfheal flowers
that cling to the wall.

The boat tilts and so does my seventy percent
of water taking the shape of its container.
Contener is two words:
con (with) and tener (to have).

To have-with. To hold together.
The outer skin marking the edge,
water is released in small, measured doses:
tears, urine, sweat.

The body as a simple container
measuring time.

≠

I went down to the water in search of a word
and all I could find was hogweed

giant hogweed
hogweed, crowding out the banks like a rainforest
hogweed, flowering white as thrush, scented as elder
hogweed, exotic in a Victorian postcard
hogweed, the only plant survivor of a nuclear holocaust

hogweed, towering above the flight of a biped
hogweed, succeeding amid harsh market conditions
hogweed, eyes upturned at the height of the argument
hogweed, cauliflower blossom-brains drying out in the sun
hogweed, standing steadfast under the chance of rain
hogweed, stuck in perma-adolescence
hogweed, homogenizing like a mono-crop
hogweed, ornamental and phototoxic
hogweed, scrolling past under the flick of a finger
hogweed, heracleum mantegazzianum
hogweed, monstera has nothing on it
hogweed, recolonizing the old world
hogweed, level-headed rebel
hogweed, reproduction unfolding ad infinitum
hogweed, calling back to the embryonic
hogweed, the end of bells around necks
hogweed, the end of bells around towns
hogweed, drawing a portrait from memory
hogweed, having the last laugh

'All the small insincerities had seeped like invisible
rivulets of acid and caused profound damages'
— Anaïs Nin, *A Spy in the House of Love*

STORY OF TWO SIDES

It was said there were two sides. One & other, two could-be brothers
misunderstanding. How did the fairytale go? Two sides and a third

blindfolded unseeing holding the scale with god or his USA
placing his heavy hand on just one of the plates

≠

It was said there were two sides. It was a two-faced two state
all the goody-two-shoes' two-cent two-to-tango in-two-minds fate

How to predicate? Eviscerate or let the other speak
of standing on your own two feet or on one phantom limb

≠

It was said there were two sides. Us and them a neatly divided
dialogue to be had between the one with roads paved in kingly stone

glowing pink and gold in evenings uninterrupted by walls
in maps unfragmented unshrinking growing even year by year

where noiseless trams transport reasonable people as if on a cloud
from one worthy endeavour to the next

from affirming brightly-lit workplaces to beautiful cafés and malls
or libraries, and books, and freedom.

One side who couldn't bear to look at itself
in the mirror of the other's pain

And the other with slow unpaved roads wedged
behind desert hills where shackled bodies

travel rammed ramshackle for two shekel a map of shards
where the unreasonable people still open their shops in the morning

even though there is nothing to sell
where the unreasonable children still go to school

even though there are no books and the school
is a pile of rubble

≠

The other hidden behind a wall

≠

It was said there were two sides until the other was no longer there
having been wiped from all records erased from all books

There were two sides until only the side of power was left

≠

(There are no two sides)
(There are no two sides)

≠

CARTOON LOVE

ON TRAVELLING TO THE CONTINENT AFTER A LONG PERIOD OF HUNGER AS A UK IMMIGRANT

The first thing I noticed upon arriving
was the provincialism of the place I came from

John Lennon stared the whole time
over my shoulder from a coffee-table book
that said 'British Style.' I replied:
I do not fear stock markets

yet I was left to continue our sad trades.
English was a cracked kettle
were we hammered the same worn tunes

THE SCIENCE OF PERAMBULATION

We choose a path through
the swarm of straw-coloured locusts.

They fly bloodwinged around your shins
bump into your blessed pilgrim toes.

You crouch through the dusty stridulation
knees creaking, hips clicking like locust.

I want to untie your sandal
wash your foot in my tears like a mystic.

You know there is abundance
in having nothing

HUNGER IN A BRITISH CITY AFTER FLEEING FROM WAR

We walk the city
and all around
blown-up
photographs of food

≠

Hunger was a time machine taking us back to when blown-up
didn't mean bombed out but instead referred to the photography
technique—a high resolution expansion filling each pixel with air
or the spaces between the granular realities of a food able to exist
both in imagination's desire and in the stomachs of passersby able
to simply purchase it, in such a way that plastering the city
with 3000000x scale pictures of ripe tomatoes, their skin covered
in dewy droplets of water, was an investment that did not offend
the eyes watering from hunger or else Blow-Up just meant
the title of an Antonioni film that was usually just perceived
as a naturalist portrayal of the swinging sixties ignoring
the plot based on a short story by Julio Cortázar
in which each subsequent zooming into
or blowing up of a photograph
brings us closer to both
the undeniability
and elusiveness
of the crime
committed in plain sight

SNOWSTORM IN EASTER

The snow came in with your words before it snowed.
It came in at 08:31 in sans serif the quick flakes whirling in
through the phone your name lit up in bold letters
and all the blank space around your name was snowdrift
rounding the inner corners or cornered by other letters

floating before my eyes was your friend's funeral down south
and the breath of the piper rising like a tent pole
to hold up silence and the drifts of people offering comfort and
the space around you burning the way hands burn
after playing in the snow for too long.

I looked up from the screen
and stared at the sun through my window, cut into four
rectangles
an afterimage of pain

≠

I gravitate outside into a puddle of sunlight, your words
still sloshing about inside me leaving behind a viscous trail
like wine's legs streaking down the curvature of the glass.
'I hope it's not snowing in Glasgow' was the message
and looking up at the blue sky it seems absurd.

Carlos Slim is talking through a wet cloth about numbers:
'1,372, which is really only
3.6 or 3.7 percent.' Why the wealthiest man
is a miser and why wealth comes with less
compassion is something I still refuse to understand. Or how

I have wanted to know solitude in such anatomic detail just
to wrap myself round friends as a cupped hand sheltering
a daisy unfurling its petals in the snowstorm that has just begun

STORY OF SNOW WHITE AT THE PALLIATIVE CARE FACILITY FOR THE TERMINALLY ILL

The hospice was so far away I never came to visit
and so it was decided without me.
These were the very last moments;
it would be a lot more convenient

to take Granny in the coffin
rather than a wheelchair, or the sickbed.
The coffin was transparent, she'd have a good view
and with the silk lining she'd be much more comfortable.

It was a beautiful day,
we rolled down the windows and opened the sunroof.
Watched the trees file down in procession and the sun
darting through the leaves.

She was quite chirpy and talked so much
I worried she might run out of oxygen inside her coffin
and die before her time.
I wanted to say something but then

if she was still alive when we got there
how would she feel as we lowered her into the ground
flowers and soil pattering onto the glass?
It was a long way to the cemetery so it was decided

we'd make a short stop to see the Joneses.
She came out of the car too,
in her glass coffin, and we all had tea and biscuits.
She didn't look ill at all. I took Dad aside and told him:

maybe it wasn't her time yet. He said no
it was just the ride
—after all a day like this
can lift anyone's spirits

YOU WOULDN'T HAVE LEFT ME IF WE LIVED IN THE FUTURE

There would have been self-cleaning dishes
and delicacies that floated, ready-made, into our mouths
after being printed at a single click.

These things have been prototyped already and will soon
be available in the mainstream market at a very low cost.
To think we were that close

and had we met a handful of years after we did
you would still be here

TO BE YOUR DOG

I doggy-paddle in the pool
looks stupid but feels good for my tailbone
to kick the scholar
in me

Out for a walk
my big headphones
round my neck
like a collar

I spot other dogs
as they seek out a scent
among the dicotyledones
ignoring their caller

We smile knowingly at each other

ROADKILL

I called my friend and asked how to lose 10lb by next Monday
for my oh so important event, she said babe it can't be done

best to love yourself but if that's too hard try eating half an apple
in the morning and half an apple at night. During the day eat
nothing

but fish flakes and plenty of water. I ate what she said lost my
ten pounds my clothes fit great. For the event I decided to wear

all black, trousers, heels and a Bardot top so I could blend into
the black curtains on stage allowing only my shoulders

and head to be seen like the floating bust of an illustrious man.
My body disappeared behind the lectern but my head was still fat.

My double chin a rolled-up blanket where I could fit a few orphans.
My haircut was somehow also fat my voice stuffed down my energy

thinned from a malnourished sense of direction and the othering
I'd learned to embrace. By then I was already roadkill a cute animal

run over by the soulless machinery of your self-hate. It hadn't
happened yet but your friends knew the discard process about to
take place

having seen you date countless foreign girls the question is
what kind of crumbtrail led me there?

please don't let on that you knew me when
I was hungry and it was your world
—Bob Dylan, 'Just Like a Woman'

STORY OF CRUMBS

Casually as opening a packet of oatcakes de dónde eres
crumbs cascading from the mouth of una persona que nunca ha
conocido another way a moción repeated mechanically
like a reflex searching context simple enough: where are you from?

How to distinguish an oatcake from a corn tostada central
to our mitología sin maíz no hay país la emplumada serpiente
followed a red ant as it carried a crumb of maize hasta donde
el maíz crecía to the Tonacatépetl of thriving

Quetzalcóatl stole the crumb and oh how it glistened I look
at the crumbs on my friends' table longingly el exceso
my first job in this country was to clear the plates
at events all the food poured into bins made my stomach churn

Desde entonces me arrepiento push my sound a la orilla
when my friends step out of the room momentarily
I press my tongue onto some crumbs still watching
the door for their return as I must not be seen doing this.

Stray crumb en el lip it is surprising how little I can be
satisfied with when even inwardly I am a guest training my mouth
to fit to the laden shapes round out vowels smooth mi dicción
try on sonidos to appear at home arrange myself in conjunction

with this foreign room whose references I am yet to decipher
my path through the crumbs of meaning languaging my way
across table the words all expertly appointed now I am stronger

≠

Q. If a woman speaks at a board meeting
and no one hears her
is there even a woman on the board?
A. I wouldn't know. I work alone

YOU WERE A MANCHILD TRAPPED IN THE BODY OF AN OLD KITCHEN CABINET

All ply polyvinyl and elegant handles you walked down the street
with your boxy chest rigid gait fixed ideas of justice and a heart
full of chipped mugs unwilling to open up for anybody.

You said things like 'excellent,', 'seems absurd I should dictate
the terms here,' in a gentle voice so as not to startle with
minute manipulations. If things weren't exactly as you wanted

the camera zoomed in on your face in mockumentary style
during uncomfortably long silences between lines of dialogue.
Finally you turned to leave and the camera

panned the whole scene as you slowly exited the frame
crestfallen, head lowered and feeling utterly misunderstood

BARBIE

We embraced, naked on your bed. You pulled off my
                Barbie head: Pop!

My body watched it dangle, your hand
                clutching the hair.

Give it back.
                What for.

I need it, give it back.

You handed it over, I
                tried but it   wouldn't fit.
        We got distracted, we   left it aside and heard it
                        roll away.

You kissed me so much I grew
another set of lips on my neck.

                I told you so, you said.

TOOTH

Tooth feels out of place does
not fit into the bite, grows
arms and legs, strange
protuberances, has
an existential crisis
wonders what if

Tooth asks what it's doing with
its life shouldn't it
be a bone or a nail instead
or grow inside an ovary would
that not be more
rewarding

Tooth unburdens itself
from its crown, refuses
to grind up food, writes
an opera libretto, weeps
while watching the news
decides to self-inmolate
I was already dead it says my
life has a continuity beyond
this mouth none of my atoms
will be destroyed I will now
be stardust

Tooth takes a microphone
sings its sorrows in slant
rhymes and assonant chords
takes the sticky blue latex
gloves staunchly

Tooth has no teeth
cannot apply the law
resolutions come late
are vetoed by the US
robes and pulpits
are non-binding

Tooth out of place
screws the device
into the gums
fingers pressing
down hard
jaw clenches
and unclenches
needle into gum

Adrenaline kicks in
making the body feel light
on the chair hands clasped
together on the lap

Tooth feeling tentatively
in language how tomorrow
scream tomorrow
in the mouth
the clutches
of sorrow and
in the teeth the
ossuary of another
time on the lips a sound

of lies gritted
between bricks
spectacles, placed
respectably
on the table

THE PROBLEM IS I DO BELIEVE MY OWN FICTIONS

Do I believe that because   I grew up in a place
where everyone around me   grew up in a place
where Walter Mercado   a queer man in a cape
read resilience in the stars   before the evening news
providing the emotional education   as our grandmas
reheated tamales for supper   and sons were better treated
than daughters and there was a hierarchy but at least
we all knew   we were part of something.

Do I believe that this made me   who I am
or do I believe that I can really   unlearn any of this
and be radically free   in a utopian void
uncorrupted by reality   do I believe my pain
my fatigue do I believe   my notebooks when I see
thought process constantly   interrupted by waves
of physical pain   and what did my therapist say?
The fuzzy feeling that falls   upon you is the part of you

trying to protect   the other part of you.
I can't remember   which part needed protection
all I know is there is a mechanism   liable to be hacked and
that everything needs to be   hacked these days

STORY OF DISCIPLINE

When I was a child, people used to say
'if a tree falls in the middle of the forest
and no one hears it,' etc.

The problem here is how we define a person
capable of hearing
if a tree is a being that does nothing but perceive.

And a community of trees—their empathy
communication and solidarity
create a kind of love is where no discipline is needed.

A pure space where intention springs
effortlessly from the ground
—a sapling in a tropical forest

where ancient canopies sweetly guard
from the birds above its tender roots
sending nourishment in a hidden neural network.

If a tree falls in the middle of the forest
the whole forest shudders, and weeps.

If I fall in the middle of the city
I still believe it is possible no one will notice
as if my interdependence with all beings were not a given.

It is a peculiar kind of arrogance
to feel that I am alone

PIET MONDRIAN

There once was a man who defended the line
in its purest and most simple state. No trying
to appear three dimensional. No secondary colours
just pure composition. To reach the most a priori
state of things. He believed in this
as a religion bored his friends with persuasions
disciplined schoolchildren according to the vertical line
and the horizontal line.

Such was his conviction that he turned his whole habitat
into a realm of geometry.
He rose in the morning
with square pillow marks on his square cheek,
pushed toothpaste from a square tube
onto a square toothbrush he'd fashioned himself,
ate square fried eggs on square toast on square white plates
adorned with lines black and straight.

≠

When he died they found in a little square box
under his square bed several hundred water-coloured flowers
each one neatly folded into four equilateral parts

STORY OF RIVERS

I woke up early today.
Blinking, I thought
of each blink as a microsecond
of being dead.
The proper dose.

Instructions to myself, written blindly
arrive to me sinusoidally through
the impossibility of unlocking muscles
to arrive at a point of relaxation
sufficient for me to understand them.

Unable to exist in this as it unfolds
caught up in the language of it
its narration. My thoughts sticky,
too similar. Run your finger against the wheat sprig
the way its tiny catches –

When asked to name my feelings
all I could find was TV static, less defined
and I was left a la orilla del amor, barfing my lungs out.
The performer need not be versed
in intonational arithmetic

How to appear sane whilst
remembering how rivers change

≠

FIRE TRIPTYCH

FIRST WE WILL LOSE IT ALL BY FIRE

For some reason we decided to live by a belief.
To stand by it even if life were to take it all away.
First we will lose it all by fire, we said.
Our house with all our possessions in it,

the territory where we reign supreme sometimes at peace
sometimes warring with one other adult.

We will lose all birdsong rainforests
vineyards and wandering
all archival records and languages whistled
mountain to mountain no ear to land in.

We will lose the songlines and opera house
the Potosí gold altarpieces, stained glass and the recipe
for how to make the colour Chartres blue.
The original, and the facsimile.

A charred fragment of a manuscript page
found in a pocket after the bombing
subsequently held in a temperature-controlled glass case
housed in a museum built on land cleared of its people –

that too will burn. Snow will be a distant memory.
We will find it curious, cruise ships where the rich may witness
the last melting glacier the polar bears thinned to starvation the
sea birds' skeletons packed with plastic knickknacks.

Then the floods, the ruined –
sailing through the city
in Versace Wellington boots.
We will speak of apocalypse horsemen

or the government's incompetence.
We will rage at words, identify their power
fixate on internet forum ortholinguistics.
Technicalities as a notion of control.

A public inquiry will take place.
The findings will come late
and change nothing.
Then we will lose it all to debt

even as the banks pour oil
on the fire. When all is gone, we said,
we will know for sure that all we ever
truly had was each other

DON'T CRY FIRE

Don't cry fire, don't claim the media
are fanning the flames don't use the words
burnout, incensed or incendio
don't describe how the baby's bones
were still hot embers underground
or mention banned chemical
weapons or the round holes
burnt through to the marrow don't utter
the striving فلسطين الشهيدة
from the river إلى البحر
no digas que arde
hasta el mar من النهر
the skin smouldering for hours or bring up
destroyed wells or rainwater illegally
collected as if the rain could be owned
don't add the only light at night
came from the flares falling slow
don't mouth arson, fierce or emboldened
don't say the Hisbeh is not in Gaza
or convey how crates of vegetables
to a crisp or the crops salvaged
from a scorched summer
don't point out temperatures are the highest
on record in a planet
already ablaze, that we can't afford
more heat don't touch on the زيتون trees
calcinated on poisoned land don't reference roots
the صمود of the opuntia or the spark
of resistance don't describe the stench
of singed hair or human
fat bubbling in the tents
of the displaced the child who howled
thick tears watching

his father melt don't say rise
from the ashes don't say love
is a burning thing or allude to the bright
in a forest of thick plumes
leave out that the firefighters
were barred from the area
avoid active verbs or subjects
responsible omit the cackle
and spit of soldiers don't assert
that settlers set or ignite
don't speak of hell or hot metal rods
or how they hissed
or jeered don't say your whole life
was up in smoke don't say pass
the torch to what orphaned child don't say
she saw in your eyes the fires
you have seen and the rage
you are asked to keep quiet

WHAT THE WITCH KNOWS

That she's drawn to the fire's glow
the smoke curling around it the nearly out
embers

The flame *tearing from the wick*
shuckling like a worshipper at the wailing
wall as if to escape itself resurrected
unheld by red glare grasping your
hand like a child's teaching you
punctuation

Death's second self the blindness
of night rivering between you like a snake

The demons awakened in you by her
presence yet to be made known
their eyes glassy from drink revealing
tenderness towards her only late
when it's time to go and there's even a taxi
waiting for you outside

Your fear of her even when she
patiently tames you

That she has no patience

That she wants to be consumed
at the stake the whole town gloating

Your poisoned return to her
hut in the woods as she stirs the cauldron
of what she is

The pricked finger to draw childhood
blood in tasting the stars

That for moments she will grow
young too

That you'd stay, and you'd block
each other's view using each other
as shields from your fate

That knowing all this she can't
ask you to stay

ONE DAY A YEAR

Tell me a thing or two about bones.
How they rise from earth like stalks
of wheat, vertebrae on vertebrae

defying gravity for a while, odds stacked
and when the breath is passed
only bones remain.

When he –
I myself was still a child
my clavicle had not yet fused to my shoulder.
Sorrows had not yet ossified between sternum and spine.

When –
Worries were barely the weight of a bird's wing.
At the faintest breeze over a field
the spirit soared.

When my son –
I remember how he lay
on my lap as I lulled him
through every toothache and fear.

When – he died –
I translated the bones
lay his head towards the river
so on waking he could meet the sunrise.

Wilfully I waited
refusing to eat or rest.
Dolor proofing like dough

filled me so I was distended.
Forgot I was still alive.

≠

Tell me how the spirit holds.
Longer than the flesh can turn it holds.
Longer than the acid in the soil dissolves

what's left and then
only memories stand
as totems we turn back to.

Today I translate the clouds.
Today I was the rain and I was starting
I was just on the edge –

≠

Each year I bake pan de muerto
for his journey back.

Laden with yolks, sweet milk and anise
getting the dough to rise is an esoteric art.

I sugar the bones. Festive bread to be lazily torn apart
over hot chocolate and shared, convivial and smiling

with those of us still here.
One day a year

NOTES

The text in 'Story of Jacob Baegart' was reworked from an extract of Baegart's 1768 *Observations in Lower California* (University of California Press, 1952), translated into English from the original German by M. M. Brandenburg and Carl L. Baumann.

The lyrics in 'Self-serve Slurpee' are inspired by my translation into English of the song 'Soy Así' by Valentín Elizalde.

The quote in 'In a Way, Enclosed by its Container Wall, the River Clyde Is' is from a 1759 Act of Parliament that gave Glasgow town councillors powers to straighten the river.

The quote in 'Story of Rivers' is from the BBC Scottish Orchestra concert notes, 13 January 2018.

'First We Will Lose it all by Fire' references a display seen in the National Museum of Israel, a short story title by Julio Cortázar ('Manuscript Found in a Pocket'), and a passage from Viktor Frankl's *Man's Search for Meaning*.

'In Springfield, Mexico, Lisa Simpson Speaks in Spanish' was commissioned by Jaime Martínez.

'Mountain Road' was commissioned by Shehzar Doja.

'One Day a Year' was commissioned by the Bamburgh Ossuary in St. Aidan's Crypt and Newcastle University for the anthology *A Hut a Byens*.

ACKNOWLEDGEMENTS

With gratitude to the editors of *Wet Grain*, *English: Journal of the English Association*, *Poetry International*, *Less: Journal of Degrowth*, and the *Terras Magia/No Magia* journal issue dedicated to Mexican poetry, for first publishing some of these poems.

Thanks to my editor Anthony Anaxagorou for his invaluable editorial input and Patricia Ferguson for the care going into this publication.

To Bertha Michel and Claire & David Rousson for providing writing retreat space; likewise to the Martínez Calleja family, Laia Jufresa, Sophie Hughes, Elian Carsenat, and Ghazal Mosadeq.

To my family in Mexico for the love and support.

To Liliana Guerra for the voicenotes keeping me company through the timezones.

To Giannoula Kounadi and Antonella Marsella for being my family in Glasgow always.

To Henry Bell for his editorial eye and pivotal suggestions on the manuscript's various iterations; to Hazem Jamjoum for his generosity in sharing his towering knowledge and encouraging me to write about Palestine; to Shehzar Doja for the collaboration that led to 'In a Way, Enclosed by its Container Wall, the River Clyde Is'; to Roxana Cortés for bringing glitter and philosophy; and to dogo (aka greum maol stevenson) for his unconditional presence and care.

Thanks are due to the Society of Authors for providing a work-in-progress grant in 2019 which supported an initial draft of this book.

SELECTED OTHER TITLES BY OUT-SPOKEN PRESS

Down • REBECCA MCCUTCHEON

Bark, Archive Splinter • JAY GAO

Boiled Owls • AZAD ASHIM SHARMA

[...] • FADY JOUDAH

Vulgar Errors / Feral Subjects • FRAN LOCK

*State of Play: Poets of East & Southeast Asian Heritage in
Conversation* • EDS. EDDIE TAY & JENNIFER WONG

Nude as Retrospect • ALEX MARLOW

Today Hamlet • NATALIE SHAPERO

G&T • OAKLEY FLANAGAN

sad thing angry • EMMA JEREMY

Trust Fall • WILLIAM GEE

Cane, Corn & Gully • SAFIYA KAMARIA KINSHASA

apricot • KATIE O'PRAY

Mother of Flip-Flops • MUKAHANG LIMBU

Dog Woman • HELEN QUAH

Caviar • SARAH FLETCHER

Somewhere Something is Burning • ALICE FRECKNALL

flinch & air • LAURA JANE LEE

Fetch Your Mother's Heart • LISA LUXX

Seder • ADAM KAMMERLING

54 Questions for the Man Who Sold a Shotgun to My Father
JOE CARRICK-VARTY

Lasagne • WAYNE HOLLOWAY-SMITH

Mutton Rolls • ARJI MANUELPILLAI

Contains Mild Peril • FRAN LOCK

Epiphaneia • RICHARD GEORGES

Stage Invasion: Poetry & the Spoken Word Renaissance
PETE BEARDER

The Neighbourhood • HANNAH LOWE

The Games • HARRY JOSEPHINE GILES

Songs My Enemy Taught Me • JOELLE TAYLOR